MARKETING MACHINE

7 MARKETING SECRETS AND WHY EXPENSIVE CONSULTANTS DON'T WANT YOU TO KNOW ABOUT THEM

ROBIN WAITE

Bestselling author of **Online Business Startup** and **Take Your Shot**

Robin Waite

THE FEARLESS BUSINESS COACH

First Published in Great Britain 2018

By Robin M. Waite

Paperback ISBN 978-0-9957768-9-0

Robin Waite Limited
Stroud House
Russell Street
Stroud
Gloucestershire
GL5 3AN

www.robinwaite.com

CONTENTS

For Charles

Some marketing tips for you inside. Be Fearless!

Robin Waite

HELP! MY MARKETING SUCKS!

You are a service business in one of the following sectors; coaching, consulting or freelancing. You exchange time for money. You want to work fewer hours and make more money in the process.

However, you are struggling with marketing and generating leads for your business. And instead of REAL marketing, you are spraying marketing shi*t all over your prospects without even realising it.

If you want to know what the *7 Business Marketing Secrets* are, and Why Expensive Marketing Consultants Don't Want To Share Them With You, then read on.

I have a disruptive way about how I go about coaching my clients. As you may have noticed, and no offence to anybody who wears a suit and has grey hair, but I'm a business coach in a t-shirt.

I believe that coaching is all about creating success while building businesses and having fun along the way.

Marketing Machine is my take on marketing, which is disruptive. I'll be throwing a lot of different ideas at you, and

I will change, not just one or two of your perceptions around marketing. But I will change ALL your perceptions and your approach to marketing.

Does that sound cool?

To explain the *7 Business Marketing Secrets*, I've invented something called the Magical Marketing Mystery Machine.

Who wants to know about the Magical Marketing Mystery Machine?

Here goes.

Enjoy!

By the way, if you read all the way to the end of this guide, there are a couple of little gifts for you at the end.

HOW TO USE THIS BOOK:

STEP 1: Read *Marketing Machine* with an open mind

STEP 2: Start implementing

STEP 3: If you get stuck, email me: robin@robinwaite.com

SECRET #1

YOU THINK THAT MARKETING IS THE FOLLOWING...

- Your website?
- YouTube videos?
- Instagram?
- Email Marketing?
- Blogging?
- Networking?
- Twitter?
- Flyer/Leaflet Drops?
- Facebook Ads?
- Etc, etc

Anyone who knows me, and has seen me speak or read previous content I've written, will know where this is going.

Marketing is none of the above, that's all bullsh*t.

Those things are **NOT** marketing; those are tools that you use in marketing.

Marketing <u>IS</u> the process of nurturing prospects once you've attracted someone's attention using the tools listed above.

Enter the Magical Marketing Mystery Machine.

The Magical Marketing Mystery Machine looks a little bit like this.

You don't know what it spits out but it's got a funnel, and you put stuff into it.

You chuck in MailChimp, YouTube, LinkedIn, Facebook, Instagram, vlogging, twitter, your website, and Facebook ads. You shove all of those into the funnel at the top.

And that creates customers, right? Every time, all the time!

You've produced all this content and put it out there, and you've got clients, that's marketing, right? No, **<u>marketing isn't any of those things</u>**. Those are just tools that we use in marketing.

The process of marketing is very different.

Marketing produces clients, every time, all the time, right?

If you remember the hopper in the previous image, that nice shiny silver hopper. Well, the hopper for most businesses looks completely different.

For 99.9% of small businesses, the hopper looks more like a muck spreader, and it sprays marketing sh*t all over potential prospects.

Most people spray marketing sh*t all over prospects

In this guide, I'm going to show you **HOW TO DO MARKETING THE RIGHT WAY.**

Why is Marketing so bloody complicated?

The answer is simple.

At the dawn of the internet age, 25 years ago, there were 460,000 registered small businesses in the UK. Today, there are 3,9m registered UK businesses.

There are no new ideas and ten times the number of people competing in your business sector.

The Internet has made marketing easy, right? Global marketplace and all that.

Rubbish! It's made it ten times harder and if you work in an industry which is based online then think 40-50 times harder to get found.

SECRET #2
YOU DON'T RESEARCH YOUR TARGET MARKET

...and just chucking out boring, vanilla, marketing sh*t.

Copywriters who earn $25,000 for a 2-page sales letter earn their money in tow ways. First by researching their client's ideal client, the target market, and the client's pain points. They also happen to be great at writing content.

For the pros, it's 80% research and 20% writing the content.

But take the copywriter's lead and **take the time to research** before putting pen to paper.

A LITTLE MARKETING 101 -

1. Identify your target market.
2. Ask the question, "Where do they hang out?
3. Go to them, i.e. make it as easy as possible for them to find you.
4. Show up **REGULARLY** and **OFTEN** with the same **CONSISTENT** message.

I'll deal with the first three points in this section, but step four deserves its own section.

Identify your target market, makes sense, you all know what that means.

Have a clear idea of who buys your products and services.

If I hear the three letter acronym 'SME' one more f*cking time, I am going to destroy that person. "My target market is SMEs!" F*CK OFF!

An 'L' Business, i.e. a business with 250+ employees is a 'Large' Business.

There are only 9,000 large businesses out of 3.9m registered businesses in the UK.

Do you know what that means?

*"EVERY BUSINESS IS A F*CKING SME!"*

That is not a **TARGET** Market; it's **ALL** the market!!!

So, be specific. Most of you working in the small business community don't need **ALL** of the clients to create a decent business with regular recurring revenue.

Identify the ten businesses who want to work with you. Don't waste your time targeting the 3.9m who don't want your stuff… or, at least don't want it right now.

Where do they hang out?

Get a bit stalky! Start to understand our clients well. I bet you don't take the time to go through the simple step of researching your ideal client.

You know absolutely nothing about your prospects, yet you start producing content.

And that's it!

They told us to do Facebook ads, and we start doing Facebook ads. We haven't taken the time to work out who we're targeting those Facebook ads at.

We chuck out a blog article; we haven't taken the time to do some research to work out who that blog article is targeting.

You show up to a business show because there are loads of business owners there but can't understand why everyone took your free sh*t and then ghosted you.

NOW!

Slooooow the process down and start to get to know your prospects better.

The third thing to remember is to GO TO WHERE YOUR TARGET MARKET HANG OUT.

Make it easy for your prospects to find you.

I'm not talking physically hanging out, but you need to have an idea about what they get up to in order be in front of them when they are ready to buy.

SECRET #3
YOU ARE NOT BEING CONSISTENT

------

1. Identify your target market.
2. Ask the question, "Where do they hang out?"
3. Go to them, i.e. make it as easy as possible for them to find you.
4. Show up REGULARLY and OFTEN with the same CONSISTENT message.

All I hear are things like:

"I tried Facebook Ads, and it didn't work for me!"

You hit the " Blue Boost Button" once and burned through fifty bucks...but got no leads? You're not an FB ad expert so I'm not surprised. I spent over £4,000 learning about FB ads before I got the hang of it and started making it work for me.

"I tried cold calling, and it didn't work for me!"

I can guarantee you called one or two people, pissed them off and then gave up. You'll get one person interested in every 70 calls you make.

"I tried Email Marketing, and it didn't work for me!

Your products target mums with school-age children, and you sent your email marketing "campaign" out at 11 am on a Tuesday morning during half-term. You're surprised it didn't work, so you don't resend it next week?

Why doesn't this work?

The answer is obvious.

We're not experts in Facebook advertising. We're not experts in email marketing or using MailChimp, or writing marketing copy, or professional bloggers.

The internet has created this virus where all this marketing stuff online is fooling us into thinking it's easy.

IT'S TOTAL BULLSH*T

"As soon as you accept the fact that Marketing is bloody hard, the easier it will become for you."

Now you can manage YOUR expectations, knuckle down and do the 2 or 3 things that **DO WORK** for marketing your business.

As a business owner, you must show up **regularly** and **often** enough (caveat: without being annoying) and with the same **consistent** message. Making sure that when your prospects are in the right mindset to buy your products that you are the one who appears front and centre at the forefront of their mind.

Don't just do the odd Facebook Ad. Learn how to do it well and do it consistently.

Don't just send one email marketing campaign and go, "Oh it

didn't work for me."

Think about this, if you're the business owner who works with parents of school-aged children. The one who sent their email out at nine o'clock on a Tuesday morning during half term.

Had you sent it the same time next week they wouldn't be on half term; they will be sat at their desk, doing a bit of work, waiting for your marketing email to arrive.

That's how email marketing works; you must be consistent with it.

Consistency is the key to winning at marketing and growing a healthy pipeline of leads.

Next up write these three numbers down:

7 Hours of Engagement

11 Touch Points

4 Locations

Remember to build ENGAGEMENT across multiple TOUCH POINTS and LOCATIONS

Seven-eleven-four stands for seven hours of engagement, eleven touch points, and four locations. I credit multiple bestselling author, Daniel Priestley, for introducing me to 7-11-4.

Most small business owners carry out their marketing around touch points.

Think about what you did when you first started your business.

You bought some business cards, maybe a brochure and a website, social media platforms, YouTube channel and got various marketing channels set up.

And then got no clients or maybe one or two.

But how many business cards did you hand out? How many videos did you upload to your YouTube channel? How many people have you invited to like your Facebook page? Did you invest time in SEO to drive people to your website?

That's a "maybe" to all those questions then.

The reality - nobody is going to buy your products or services unless they've had seven hours of engagement with you.

You've got to expose yourself to prospects…erm, sorry! But you know what I mean!

I'm not making these numbers up. Google did a study with all their gazillion bits of data. It's now in a book called *Zero Moments of Truth*. Google says that if we don't engage prospects for seven hours, it's unlikely they will buy from us.

Imagine this scenario; you go to a networking event, you've got a business card, you talk to somebody for five or ten minutes at the event, and you exchange business cards.

Afterwards, you go and have a look at their website if you can find it. Then you browse their LinkedIn profile.

That's four touchpoints, but…

Business cards create 15 seconds of engagement, max. You've got the five or ten-minute conversation. The average time of engagement people spend on websites is two and a half minutes. And then maybe if they scroll down your LinkedIn profile, probably not seeing anything of interest in there.

That's a maximum of 15-minutes engagement. Nowhere near that seven hours of engagement that Google and Dan Priestley encourage us to create.

I focus my marketing around things like speaking engagements, podcast interviews and book. With a speaking gig, I'm in front of 100+ people. If you're in the audience, I suppose you could walk out of the room if you wanted to, but I've got you for the next half an hour.

If you read one of my books, some of you probably already have or are doing so now. Take Your Shot is about an hour and a half to read, two hours maybe if you're a bit slow. Then you get into my YouTube channel for 30-40 minutes. Perhaps you'll complete my assessment form and book a 30-minute Diagnostic Call.

No money has exchanged hands up to now.

However, I've built up several hours of engagement with very little investment of time per prospect. You'll have more trust and commitment with me than other business coaches.

Now if you're looking for a business coach, who are you likely to turn to? Me of course, I am the best business coach, after all.

SECRET #4
YOU ARE MEASURING THE WRONG KPI

"If you measure success on sales, then you have FAILED.

If you're measuring how many conversations you're having and prospects you're nurturing, then you are WINNING."

How do you go about the engagement process?

Marketing is **NOT** about the content and the tools we use. A little clue right here >>> **ENGAGEMENT is what marketing is about.**

Marketing is all about the process of nurturing your prospects, and the customer journey you lead them through. One thing is standing out from the crowd; the second problem occurs when you drop the ball as a human being and business owner. And you WILL drop balls.

Yes, there's content creation and marketing. But what you've got to do is convert the content that you're putting out and turn it into conversations.

When a client or a prospect puts their hand up and says, "I'm interested." You immediately drop the ball. What do you do? You ignore them. You do nothing with the lead. You will subconsciously say, "I don't know what to do next!" because you don't have any systems in place to deliver a marketing asset to your prospect automatically. You don't have the brochure or a copy of Take Your Shot to give to prospects.

If you don't have any assets to be able to give to a prospect, then give someone else's marketing asset to them as a gift. Just provide them with something.

When a prospect says, "I like that post you wrote." You will reply immediately with, "That's cool, if you want to know more about that, I've got this free 42-page PDF guide for you to download and read" Or, "I've got this ten-minute video, which will help you through that challenge that you've got in your business.".

It comes down to this:

"Most people have some form of intelligence, right? We hope. When it comes to your products and services, they have none."

You must take them by the hand and lead them through the customer journey for your products and services. What's obvious to you won't be evident to your prospects.

Next up we introduce the human element into your customer journey.

Take it offline.

If any of you think that you can solely do business online these days - just because the internet has made marketing easy - it's all bullshit.

People still buy from people.

Marketing is turning full circle, and it's coming back to people wanting to sit down with other people and have face to face human contact. We are pack animals at the end of the day. And now we are sceptical of all this online marketing nonsense that's out there.

Everyone is a f*cking guru nowadays and quite frankly, as a small business owner, you are more intelligent than that.

And then finally…

Finally…

After the end of having created seven hours of engagement, plus those eleven touch points, across multiple different locations, you've earned the right to ask for some money in exchange for your products or services. That happens at the end. That builds loyal customers who come back and buy time and again from you.

Here is the second set of numbers that I want you to write down, please.

70 - Calls

10 - Appointments

2 - Sales

The magic formula for every service business = 70-10-2

By the way, these numbers live on my wrist 24/7 as a reminder of the volume of activity I MUST PRODUCE **<u>EACH AND EVERY DAY</u>** to grow my business.

70-10-2 is the second set of numbers that came out of *Zero Moments of Truth.*

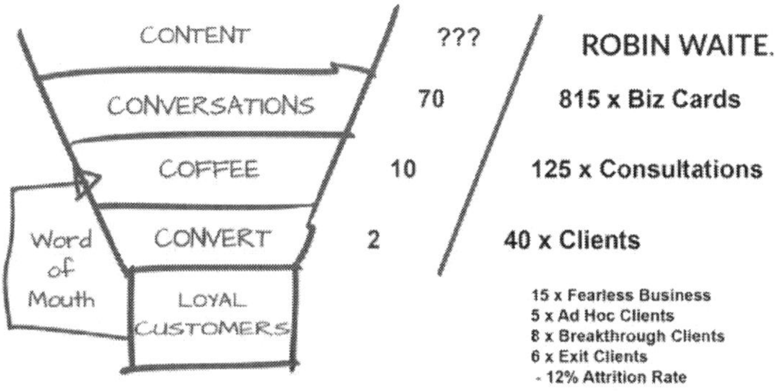

70 Conversations, 10 Coffee Meetings, 2 Conversions

A sale is a **<u>LAG</u>** indicator. If your target is two new clients per month, and you get to the end of the month having created one new client, there is nothing you can do to influence this up or down. The horse has bolted.

But...

Measure **LEAD** indicators and if, halfway through the month, you've generated 20% of the leads you need to create two sales...you can up the volume of activity in your marketing and produce the extra 80% of leads.

"Measure LEADS and NOT JUST sales."

I am confident, that like most business owners you are focussing on the number down at the bottom - the two sales. Turnover, sales, and profit determine the key performance indicators (KPIs) in your business.

Who agrees that those are the right KPIs?

The reason why they're the wrong KPIs is that by the time you review those KPIs, you have no way of influencing that number up or down. Imagine you're doing an annual review, you cannot control the past. You are now reacting and not being proactive in your business.

Whereas if you're reviewing the KPIs on a monthly or even weekly basis; you can pivot and adapt your activity levels accordingly.

By measuring the leads, you may get six months through the year, and that number is only ten out of your targeted 70 conversations. At this point, it's unlikely we're going to hit your KPI of 2 sales.

You've now got two choices:

- Pivot and produce more activity – raise your game – and force the numbers up.
- Sit back and fail.

You need to start measuring your leads.

Has that changed your perceptions about the volume of activity you're doing in your business right now from a marketing perspective?

It's vital that we measure ALL numbers. Lead and Lag. Now, I don't want any excuses. I don't want you to turn around and say, "But I'm not a numbers person." Again, that's bullshit; you cannot own a small business and not know about the numbers in your business, marketing, sales activities, how the accounts and the bookkeeping work to at least be able to tell somebody else how to do it.

You're doing yourself a disservice if you don't understand even a little bit about the mechanics of marketing in your business.

"You cannot use excuses like I'm not into numbers. It doesn't fly with me, that's not a business owner."

I know my numbers. In 2017 I collected 815 business cards from various speaking gigs. I booked 125 consultations, and I created 40 clients. 15 of those were in my group programme, I had five ad-hoc clients, eight breakthrough clients, and six clients started and completed my coaching programme.

I have an attrition rate of 12%. I know that on a weekly basis if I sit one Diagnostic Call per week, my business stays where it is.

When I sit two Diagnostic Calls per week my business grows.

It's a very simple metric. All I've got to do is fill up those Diagnostic Call slot.

Why don't you book one now?"

Is this changing your approach to marketing? And how you measure it?

Good.

This stage in *Marketing Machine* is where it's going to get interesting.

WHAT SORT OF THINGS MUST YOU WRITE ABOUT WHEN MARKETING YOUR BUSINESSES?

SECRET #5
YOU'RE NOT BEING BRAVE WITH YOUR CONTENT

Quite frankly most of the content I see on LinkedIn, Facebook, blogs and YouTube is just plain dull.

How many of you read a headline and yawn, "Not another one of those posts!" In fact, most of them don't have a headline, and they expect you just to read it.

Even if you do read it, because one of your associates or contacts in an engagement pod wrote it, you're left feeling a bit flat.

The answer? Find some fresh and exciting stuff to write about.

I do tend to steer away from tactical stuff, but I'm going to show you some tools now in this handy guide. These are practical things you can do right now, starting today that's going to change the way you do marketing

The first tool I want you to look at is https://answerthepublic.com

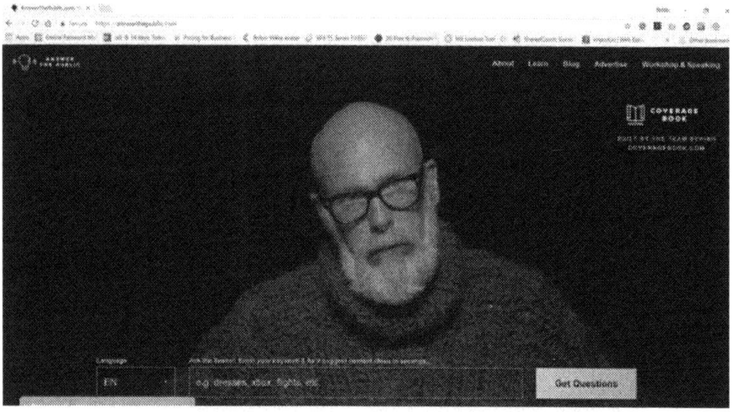

Pop your search term, maybe your industry or business sector, into Answer The Public.

Let's take "business coach" as an example.

You all know the search suggestions which appear when you start typing something into Google. The search suggestions are based on what people are searching for around your industry. Answer the Public uses this data to drive its suggestion engine.

Most of us think we know our clients; we don't stop and research to work out exactly what it is that they're searching. Most of the time it's very different to *what we think our prospects are searching.*

In the image on the following page here are some examples of what people are searching for around the topic of a Business Coach.

"Who's is the best business coach in the world?"

"Where to find a business coach?"

"What can a business coach do for you?"

"How much does a business coach cost?"

"Why do you need a business coach?"

Questions raised using answerthepublic.com

These are real questions prospects want an answer. They want to know extra information about a business coach before they make their buying decision. The answer to the first question is obvious by the way.

The search suggestions are an excellent opportunity to get to know your audience.

Where it got interesting for me, for the term business coach, is around my niches.

Who here struggles to niche? Do you know what your niche is? Well, this gave me about twenty.

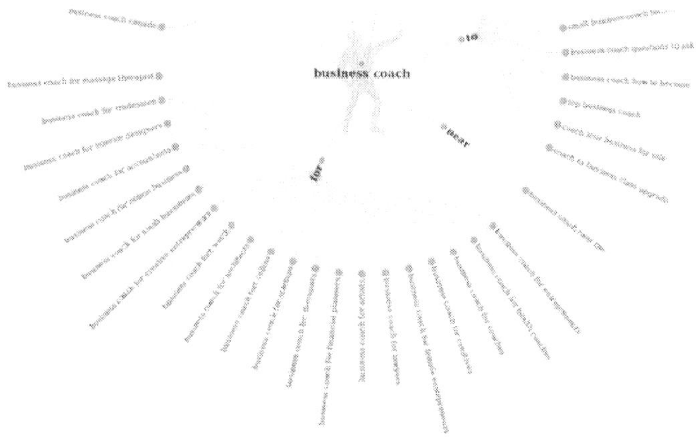

Struggling to niche? Look at the prepositions on answerthepublic.com

It delivered the following; business coach for:

- massage therapist
- tradesman
- interior designers
- accountants
- online business
- small businesses
- etc. etc.

This one search took me about 20 seconds. I got a whole host of information about what people are searching for online around the topic of a "business coach".

Answer The Public is a free tool, so use it.

Next up, what content do you need to be writing?

"Sell them what they need not what they want?" Yeah, again, more bullshit we are fed.

In your marketing message tell people about the remarkable outcome you're going to deliver for them right from the off.

If you work with me, in my intensive coaching programme, I'll help you to double your turnover within six months. Some of you cynics out there will be thinking you're not sure whether I can deliver that result. However, I've got case studies and testimonials to back that big, hairy, bold promise up.

You are likely one of the people who is too afraid to big yourself up and shout about the great work that you do for your clients and customers.

I have one single goal in mind when I work with my clients now. I get my clients to a point where they have so much confidence in their products or services that they can offer 100% money back guarantee without worrying about it.

They are that confident in the outcome that they can deliver. Are you?

Talk about it in your marketing message. Don't make false promises. Don't lie. Tell your prospects what you've done for your clients and customers. Better still get your customers to leave reviews for you and make videos telling prospects how great you are

You are a great business owner. You run a great business. So, tell people about it.

"Market to what people want. They don't buy features; they buy results."

Then sell them what they want. Again, this doesn't involve selling a feature-set. Think about it another way; all the way through your customer journey your prospects are thinking, "What's in it for me?"

During the marketing campaign, customer journey and finally the sales pitch deliver clarity and confidence in your products. Transparency and trust that you can provide that remarkable outcome, it's simple, isn't it?

The mistake that most people make is to go straight into feature selling in **ANY AND ALL** content that they push out. Next time you're trawling through your LinkedIn feed look at the structure of the posts. They are all about the features of the person's products or services. YAWN!

Now I could tell you that my coaching programme requires us to meet once a month for two hours, that there's a Facebook Group for accountability, and webinar Q&A session and this that and the other, but the reality is you're not interested in that. Because you're all sat there thinking, "What's in it for me?"

For pretty much all your prospects their biggest problem will be one, or more of the following, they:

- want more money
- have a desire to save money
- want more time
- have a problem or a pain point that needs removing

- can't do it themselves
- don't have the time to do it themselves

Talk about the opposite. The opposite being the opposite of their biggest problem. And the opposite of their biggest problem is the most likely outcome. Sell your prospects using clarity and confidence around that outcome and then finally. Finally, **you get to deliver the features** of your products or services.

You will deliver what they need plus the awesome outcome you promised them in the first place. Tell your prospects what you're going to do for them, do it and then tell them what you did. It's so obvious, in fact, that you shouldn't even need to tell them what you did. Is this all making sense?

HOW DO YOU GO ABOUT WRITING ENGAGING CONTENT?

There's a straightforward formula in copywriting called AIDA.

It's a simple framework (not mine):

A - Attention

I - Interest

D - Desire

A - Action

Each piece of content you write should contain these four

principles. ALL OF THEM! Regardless of whether you write four sentence posts on Facebook or 800-word articles on LinkedIn

“And tell stories, for goodness sakes. Let’s not make this all about you and your bloody products.”

Shout about your wins with clients.

FIRSTLY, ‘A’ STANDS FOR ATTENTION.

When I mentioned the Magical Marketing Mystery Machine, it piqued your interest, right?

I’ve got you hooked, and hopefully, you’ll now be engaged enough to read the next sentence that I write. If I’m relatively entertaining, you’ll stick with me.

Create attention-grabbing headlines to give people a reason to read on.

Think of the very cliched and overused power drill analogy. Why do people go into B&Q to buy a drill?

No!!!

It’s not to drill a f*cking hole; it’s not even to put a screw into the wall, bang the rawl plug-in or screw the bracket up; it’s probably to hang a picture or TV on the wall.

It’s not about the picture, it’s about the content in the picture, and the emotion that picture draws out the person looking at it. Imagine that picture is a piece of artwork you inherited from a dead relative. When you look at the painting, it reminds you of when your Grandfather showed you the picture when you were six years old. It provokes an emotional response. A happy memory.

IT'S NOT ABOUT THE DRILL.

Do you see how far I took that analogy? Most people in marketing, coaches and consultants, don't even get close to why we buy the drill.

Now, you've got to always think about **the benefit behind the benefit** in your business, that you create for your prospects.

The drill and hole are, "I'm going to save you time or I'm going to save you money." Deep down though, think about your purchasing habits. What does that mean to you?

I've worked with a client and helped them move from £1,000/mth revenue to over £4,000/mth in revenue within twelve months. *It's not about the money.* As a family with their two young children, they can now start thinking about putting aside a significant amount of money for a deposit on their next house.

"It's not about the business. It's not about the money; it's about the house. That's the benefit behind the benefit for them."

Whenever you start to think about your prospects needs, go deep and keep on digging even further. Build these benefits into your headlines.

There are some fantastic tools which I've found to help you formulate those attention-grabbing headlines to help you along the way. Most of you will read posts which are about, "The Top Ten Tips for XYZ" and likely think to yourself, "Here we go, yet another one of those posts!"

The reality is that person's thought about who their target market is and the fact that if the headline doesn't entice you to read you probably don't need the solution the author is offering. If the post is about the "Top 10 Email Marketing Tips" and you are sat there thinking, "Oh not another one of those posts!" it's not because of the headline it's because you're not interested Email Marketing right now. Or maybe you are, but your problem isn't big enough that you need help solving it...yet!

Portent's Content Idea Generator is a great tool. Pop your search term into Portent, and it throws back headlines in four parts. You can keep on hitting refresh, and it'll keep creating interesting headlines for you.

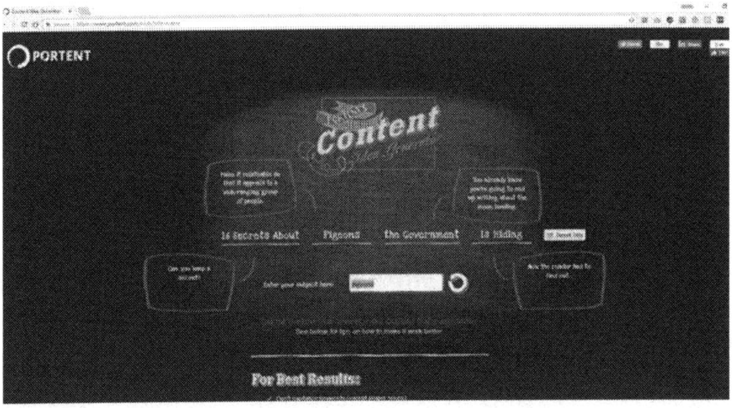

Portent's Content Idea Generator is Amazing!

Headlines like:

- How to build an empire with a business coach.
- Seventeen BS facts about web design that everyone thinks are true.
- Sixteen Secrets About Pigeons the Government Is Hiding.
- Unbelievable Shiatsu Success Stories

Even if you're not interested in pigeons you're intrigued at least, right?

Imagine pigeons which are employed by the government with tracking devices and cameras attached to them, watching your every move. And what's weirder is that pigeons are everywhere aren't they, watching us.

Do you see what I did there?

I told a story. Interested to read more? More than likely.

You've just got to get the structure of the headline right. A headline that's catchy and amusing and powerful that intrigues the reader to dive into the article.

Shiatsu I know nothing about. "Shiatsu Success Stories" I'm unlikely to read that. But "**UNBELIEVABLE** Shiatsu Success Stories". Now I'm interested.

Drop a few power words into your headlines, like "unbelievable", "secrets", "amazing" and so on. The word 'unbelievable' captures one's imagination

"Sixteen secrets the government is hiding", it's quite powerful bold statement.

Check this resource out if you want a list of AWESOME POWER WORDS:

Power Words >>> https://ninjaoutreach.com/words-to-write-better-headlines/

This tool is bloody brilliant, thank me later: Title Generator >>> http://www.title-generator.com/

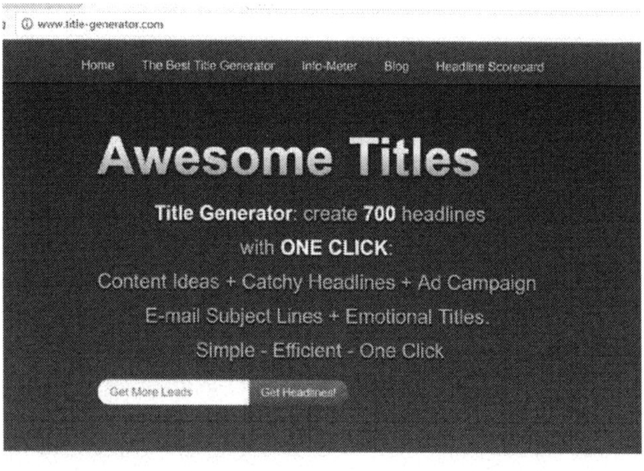

I kid you not; Title Generator gives you 700 headlines in one click, it's obscene.

I searched for "Lead Generation" which produced the following headlines...

- 3 Things Everyone Knows About Lead Generation That You Don't
- The Ultimate Secret of Lead Generation
- You Don't Have to Be a Big Corporation to Start Lead Generation
- You Can Thank Us Later – 3 Reasons to Stop Thinking About Lead Generation
- Find Out Now, What Should You Do To Create Leads Fast
- Top 3 Ways to Get More Leads
- Congratulations, Your Lead Generation Strategy is About to Become Obsolete
- Turn Your Lead Generation Campaign Into A High Performing Machine
- The Philosophy of Lead Generation
- World Class Tools to Make Lead Generation Easy

And...

- The Secret to Lead Generation
- 15 Lessons About Lead Generation You Need to Learn to Success
- Take 10 Minutes to Get Started With Lead Generation
- What You Should Have Asked The Gurus About Lead Generation
- Best Lead Generation Apps
- 15 Unheard Ways to Achieve Great Lead Generation Success
- The Ultimate Guide to Lead Generation

Plus 682 other brilliant suggestions!!!

Right then, how many of you use stock photos? Come on fess up. Right, no more of those bland stock photos, where all the people in the photo are wearing suits while standing in a skyscraper, and they're shaking hands. The pic is a blue hue.

I will upchuck if I see another stock photo like that again.

Come on people. It's time to get more creative about the imagery which you use.

The images and headline that you choose to use are what's going to hook people in and read your content. And again, there are loads of silly little tools out there to help you create fun and engaging images.

Break Your Own News is a personal favourite of mine. You punch in a headline in the ticker, and you end up with a fantastic graphic that you can use in social media.

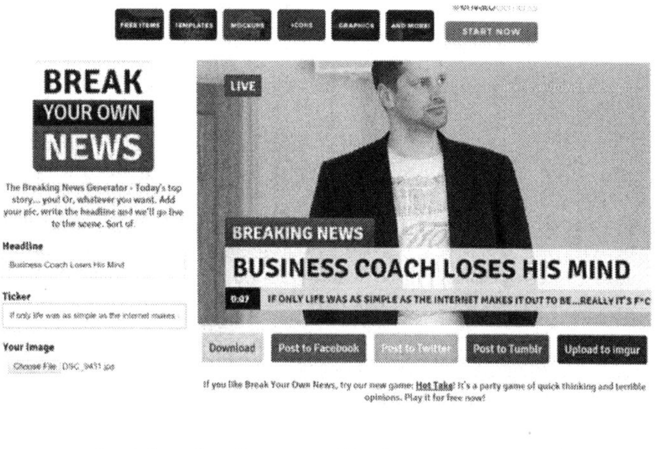

Break Your Own News - http://breakyourownnews.com/

This image would draw you in or create even a little bit of intrigue, right? It's newsy looking – that's a word by the way – and already has some social proof because this is what news stories look like.

I can see there's going to be fifty posts this afternoon of people who've been in the news. Moral of the story; if you overuse it people WILL get bored. You've got to mix it up a little bit.

There's some cool stuff that you can do on Instagram. Rather than posting up single images; I've seen a lot of people chopping up images into four blocks, and then as the Instagram tiles get laid up the four images make up a full picture in the feed.

Especially if you've got a brand which pops out can make your Instagram feed look interesting.

NOW YOUR HEADLINE IS GREAT. WHAT NEXT?

Interest! You've got to pique someone's **INTEREST**.

Just to let you know, you're screwed at this point if you can't write for toffee.

Just kidding!

But the reality is the moment you reader gets bored; they're going to disappear.

Each sentence MUST lead the reader into the next sentence, and the following sentence…and the following sentence. The purpose of every sentence is to get them to read the next one.

I had a challenge in my Fearless Crew Members Group that I called The Fearless Post.

The idea for this came from me receiving a cold email from somebody. I don't usually get riled by spam but, for some reason, this one got me particularly angry. My gut instinct told me to reply. So, I responded to it, and I gave the guy ten tips on what he should've written in his email… and then shared it on LinkedIn, as one does.

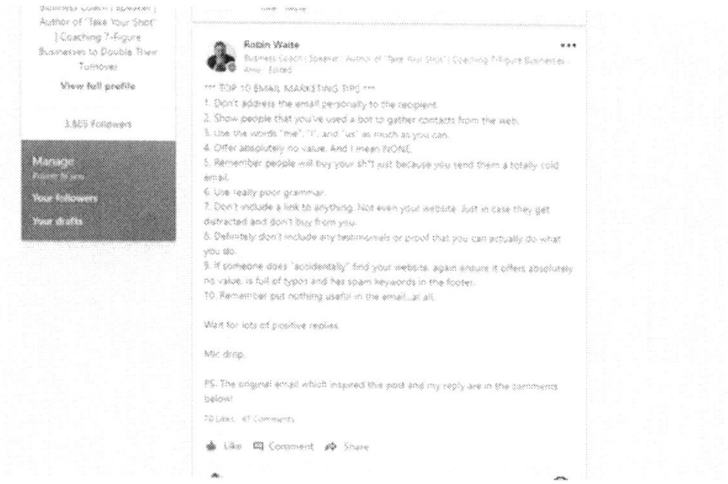

The headline was *** TOP TEN EMAIL MARKETING TIPS ***.

Are you interested in that? You'd read it right? Certainly if you're into email marketing.

1. Don't address the email personally to the recipient.
2. Show people that you've used a bot to gather their contact info from the web.
3. Use the words me, I, and us as much as you can.
4. Offer absolutely no value, and I mean no value.

5. Use terrible grammar.
6. Remember people will buy your sh*t just because you sent them a cold email.
7. Don't include a link to anything, not even your website, just in case they get distracted and don't buy from you.
8. Definitely don't include any testimonials or proof that you can actually do what you say you can do.
9. If someone 'accidentally' finds your website, again ensure it offers absolutely no value, is full of typos and has spam keywords in the footer.
10. Remember, put nothing useful in the email...at all.

I was naming all the biggest mistakes people can make in email marketing. The idea being that I want you as the reader to react to each one of the tips in turn.

I want people to have an emotional reaction to my content, even if it's merely, *"Mmm, yes, I did that in my last email marketing campaign."*

It turned out this guy was a really bright 21-year-old YouTuber

It turned out this guy was a really bright 21-year-old YouTuber who was earning £80k a year through YouTube. I listened to my gut, and when I got his cold email, I could see the naivete in the email which he sent to me. We've since chatted a couple of times, and he's an awesome guy. Driving a Range Rover that I want. Which brings me onto **DESIRE**. Funny enough.

Heaven if you do buy my product, but hell if you don't...

DESIRE IS ALL ABOUT...

"Heaven if you do, hell if you don't!"

Hell if you don't = if you don't buy my product, this is what's going to happen.

As an example; I delivered a talk in front of 120 third-year business students at a local university. The talk was about innovation, and so I walked them through The 3 Steps of Market Research.

STEP ONE - WHAT'S THE IDEA AND DOES ANYBODY ELSE THINK IT'S A GOOD IDEA?

The 'victim' I chose during my talk had this brilliant idea for a product you pop in your mouth. It connects to your smartphone and tells you how clean your teeth are when you've finished brushing your teeth. A very cool idea and about 80 people in the audience agreed and kept their hands up.

STEP TWO - ATTACH A MONETARY VALUE TO THE IDEA.

I did a Dutch auction, and we ended up with about 20 people who would be willing to part with £50 for this product. Cool. It stands up to the second step in market research.

IN COMES STEP THREE - HEAVEN IF YOU DO AND HELL IF YOU DON'T.

If you don't buy my products, one of your teeth is going to fall out in the next 30 days. How much will you pay for it now?

Ten people still had their hands up by the time I had reached £2,000.

Heaven if you do hell if you don't. That's about building desire. I've got to have this product, and the price is irrelevant. The Heaven If You Do is also known as the Value Proposition.

WHAT ABOUT THE FINAL STEP IN AIDA...ACTION?

Imagine how many posts you've read recently. All the way down to the bottom of the page.

"Cracking headline, you're engaged, oh gosh I want the thing... oh! Erm, what do I do next?"

I'll leave a comment, or I'll share it, or like it maybe...I wanted more. And for most people, there'll be a comment or share or a like, and we will do absolutely nothing with it. And comments, likes and shares are worthless. Yeah, you can build an audience in Facebook Ads Manager...but then what?

GIVE YOUR READER A VERY SPECIFIC ACTION TO DO AT THE END OF YOUR CONTENT. SIMPLE!

It could be any of the following:

- a limited time offer
- download a PDF guide
- complete my lead magnet
- go and watch this video
- here's a short form or quiz I want you to fill out
- visit my website
- join my FB Group
- etc. etc

It could be any number of different things. 90% of people are too British to ask for something by way of a call to action. So, be un-British and lead your prospects onto the next step in your customer journey.

Focus on those who love your content.

You've created great results for your clients, SO SHOUT ABOUT THEM.

Can you double someone's turnover in 6 months?

Then TELL PEOPLE about it.

Can you change people's lives?

Then tell stories about the lives you've changed...

Hate the VAT man, then write about it.

Do you know 16 Secrets About Pigeons that the Government Don't Want You To Know...

WRITE ABOUT IT!

SECRET #6

YOU HAVE NO NURTURE SEQUENCE OR SYSTEMS

Simply put, if you've got no systems and rely on your brain you will FAIL!

How do I remember to do it? I use ToDoIst.

ToDoIst sends me an email at 5 am every morning, with a list of the tasks I've got to do that day. My PA is a part of the secret sauce behind my systems and automation in my business.

Then all I must do is add Tasks into ToDoIst like:

- Post to LinkedIn every weekday
- Upload Instagram Photo daily
- Record a YouTube video every three days

Since I started using AIDA to construct my content, I don't need to have content like pre-automated in things like Buffer.

Automation, IMHO ultimately spits out dull, boring and vanilla content.

All I've got to do is remember to post on LinkedIn using the AIDA formula, and I can write great engaging content every time.

BE CONSISTENT PEOPLE – HERE IS HOW I DO IT

1. Download ToDoIst - https://todoist.com/
2. Set up reminders on a daily, weekly or monthly basis i.e.
   "Post to LinkedIn daily", "Upload Instagram Photo every 2 days", "Record YouTube video every 3 days"
3. Make a note of your headlines and add them into the comments box on the activity on ToDoIst
4. All you've got to do is remember to click on the "View in ToDoIst" link in the daily email summary.
5. Do this for 30-60 days to form a habit of producing regular content.

Remember this is an **18-MONTH JOURNEY** to raise your profile and ensure you have created lots of evergreen content, which can work for you whilst you sleep.

There are no quick wins. This is the best way of generating organic leads consistently.

ToDoIst is a fantastic productivity tool

I write content when I'm feeling inspired, and when I feel like I can inspire you. Don't use automation systems. Please, if you can avoid them. If it's for events then fair enough. Events are time limited to a specific date, and time, therefore, it's easier to automate reminders for that type of content.

To properly engage prospects write content specifically for them. Promise to deliver a specific outcome.

SO, HOW DO I SYSTEMATISE IT?

Those who have worked with me will fill out my Assessment Form first (built using TypeForm). Then it uses Zapier to squirt the data into Insightly. Insightly is a Customer Relationship Management (CRM) tool where I manage all of my prospects and contact information.

"Remember, marketing is all about the follow-up sequence."

The customer journey is not about chucking content out there and then forgetting to follow up. So, TypeForm, Zapier and Insightly are the first steps in my engagement process. They are **INTEGRAL to my marketing**.

If you fill out my assessment form (https://robinwaite.com/assessment), it creates a contact, an organisation and an opportunity in Insightly automatically.

Some of my other favourite productivity tools

It also invites you to sign up to my list in MailChimp with a GDPR compliant double opt-in. I know you love GDPR.

I've automated all those processes.

Next up, it creates six tasks in Insightly to remind me to follow up with those new prospects. I don't drop balls. I can give you a great example of how this worked for me recently.

Three people filled out my assessment, and so they were in Insightly as opportunities but hadn't booked their consultation. Now before, and how many of you will have dropped the ball at this point? I'd have, not even dropped the ball but most likely lost the ball in a hedge somewhere if it relied on my brain.

I would've forgotten about touching base with the prospect. I meant to send you that thing, oh you didn't book, oh yeah, we'll make excuses.

I emailed my three prospects at 10.30pm in the evening using a templated email in Insightly. It took me 2 minutes. By the morning two had booked their diagnostic call. The third booked a couple of days later. Two are now clients.

"Marketing is about the whole customer journey. Increasing our conversion rates. The customer journey to the sale. Not the content we put out."

I've been working on Marketing Funnels with several clients recently, and the following appears to be a generic funnel that works across the board for most small businesses.

I've put a sample Marketing Funnel on the next page.

The only downside is that whilst this funnel looks relatively straightforward it requires some technical knowledge to implement. Most people think marketing happens on the front end through social media etc, however it's the full nurture sequence which makes marketing work.

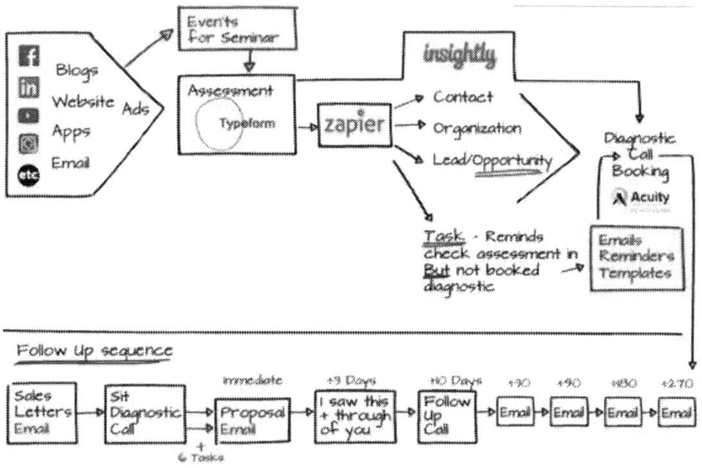

This is the nurture sequence once a lead has been generated

SECRET #7
YOU DON'T SPEND ANY MONEY ON MARKETING

Not spending on marketing is a huge mistake! You should be spending 15-20% of yourTURNOVER on marketing activities.

Most people don't spend on marketing because they fear what will happen if, "It doesn't work!"

You get the picture.

Who wants to know about the marketing minibus?

Yeah okay. I teased you with that one. See what I did there? Built a bit of desire. On second thoughts, no I'm not going to tell you about my marketing minibus.

Imagine you have a core product worth £10,000.

Then imagine I drive a funky looking minibus.

In my minibus, I've got ten of your perfect clients. They've all got black satchels full of cash. And I'm going to go and get them from my minibus, bring them in here, and they're going to empty their cash all over your table

You've just got to give me some money. How much are you

going to give me?

That's ten clients worth £10,000 each. I want you all to think about this. What would your answer be?

The Marketing Minbus

Most people say 10%.

Wrong, I'm taking my business elsewhere thank you.

Jon offered me 20%, so I'm going to drive my marketing minibus over to him, thank you very much.

My normal commission rate is about 15% so that you know.

Here's the question, "How many of you spending 15% of your turnover on marketing activities now?"

Typically, fewer than 10% of my audiences are spending this much of their turnover on marketing and wonder why they are struggling to get clients. It's not about spending the money though; there is some science behind it.

Once you've found the two or three things that work for your business from marketing perspective, then turn up the volume, on your budget for marketing, on those two or three activities that get you the clients regularly and often.

The marketing mix (i.e. those two or three things) that works for me will be different to your marketing mix. That's why I haven't gone into the marketing mix today because it isn't for everybody.

In short, most people are afraid to spend money on marketing because, as we all know the minibus doesn't exist. We don't have the guaranteed outcome at the end of our marketing activities.

And here's the kicker...you can spend a heap of cash on so-called marketing gurus, and you'll get the results, right?

WRONG!

Some are good, some get lucky, but all you are doing is giving them the cash to do what you are probably doing anyway.

Trial and error your way to working out what makes up your marketing mix.

The uber-expensive marketing "expert" is just better and more efficient at trial and error their way to a result.

CAVEAT: This is a purposefully challenging statement, there are plenty of great marketing experts who can help you, but do your research and ensure you're getting a great outcome from your investment.

If there's something which we know engages our prospects and raises the chances, the odds of us getting those clients we just got to turn the volume up on it.

"Bite the bullet! Be Fearless!"

BONUS #1
DAILY MARKETING CHECKLIST

How to use this checklist:

- 1. Set a timer for 30 minutes.
- 2. Pick a number from one to fifty.
- 3. Do the corresponding item on the checklist.
- 4. Repeat steps 2 & 3 until the clock runs down or you run out of steam.

You don't have to do EVERY item EVERY day, just do what you can, what you feel like, and if you do some of these things each and every day consistently you will start to see an improvement in your online profile.

My 5 Tips to Win at Marketing:

Show up **REGULARLY** and **OFTEN** with the same **CONSISTENT** message. And you will start to win at Marketing.

It NEVER GETS ANY EASIER , you just get better at it.

Plan to GIVE AWAY 3x more value than you would like back.

When you find your unicorn then DOUBLE DOWN on your efforts.

Decide on who THE FUTURE YOU is, and ask a simple question, "What would they be doing right now?"

Ready to get going? OK then, let's do this...

DAILY MARKETING CHECKLIST #1:

Helpareporter.com

Check what HARO (helpareporter.com) requests have filled your inbox today and reply to at least one of them.

DAILY MARKETING CHECKLIST #2:

LinkedIn Connections

Request to connect with 10 people on LinkedIn who are specifically in your target market. I've found it's easier to go to the last person you connected with and see who is a 2nd degree connection in their "people also viewed" section.

DAILY MARKETING CHECKLIST #3:

Upload a Video

Upload a 3-4 minute video to your YouTube channel. Make sure that video is SEO optimised using either TubeBuddy or VidIQ.

DAILY MARKETING CHECKLIST #4:

rev.com

If you've already got a YouTube channel, get your videos transcribed using Rev.com and use the transcription as the body of a blog article.

DAILY MARKETING CHECKLIST #5:

Facebook Pixel

Install the Facebook Pixel on your website and build the 3 basic audiences - watch this video if you need help doing this.

DAILY MARKETING CHECKLIST #6:

Ask for a Google Review

Go and ask 3 people for a Google Review. Use the Whitespark Google Review URL Generator to create a simple review link to send people. You could shorten that URL using https://bit.ly and SMS it to clients.

DAILY MARKETING CHECKLIST #7:

Leave a LinkedIn Recommendation

Leave one of your LinkedIn connections a Recommendation, you could also request a recommendation from one of your clients.

DAILY MARKETING CHECKLIST #8:

Google My Business

Spend some time optimising your Google My Business listing. This video here will walk you through the three things you need to do in order to optimise your Google My Business Listing!

DAILY MARKETING CHECKLIST #9:

Acuity Scheduling

Make it easier for clients and prospects to book a meeting with you using Acuity Scheduling.

DAILY MARKETING CHECKLIST #10:

Explainer Video

Create a 30 second explainer video using a tool like InVideo.

DAILY MARKETING CHECKLIST #11:

Facebook Friends

Add 10 friends on Facebook (yes to your personal profile) who sit within your ideal client avatar.

DAILY MARKETING CHECKLIST #12:

#PRRequest #JournoRequest

Keep an eye on the #JournoRequest tag on Twitter - more experts asking for guest contributions to articles, blogs, magazine, podcasts and TV. You can also try #PRRequest.

DAILY MARKETING CHECKLIST #13:

Facebook Groups

Jump into 5 relevant Facebook Groups and reply to 10 questions posed by members of the group. If people interact, dive in and start a conversation with them.

DAILY MARKETING CHECKLIST #14:

Medium

Take one of your existing blog articles and upload it to https://medium.com.

DAILY MARKETING CHECKLIST #15:

Write a Blog Article

Write a blog article. If you're struggling for ideas then try out a search on Answer the Public or Ripp.ly. If you're struggling for time then why not engage a Blog Writing Service like FatJoe.

DAILY MARKETING CHECKLIST #16:

Email Newsletter

Send out an email newsletter to your marketing list. If you don't have a mailing list yet maybe think about signing up to an email marketing tool such as MailChimp, ConvertKit, ActiveCampaign or something similar.

DAILY MARKETING CHECKLIST #17:

Guest Podcasts

Write to 5 podcast hosts who are in a similar niche to your own and see if they are accepting guest applications. Why not also check out the Fearless Business Podcast while you're at it ;-)

DAILY MARKETING CHECKLIST #18:

Connect on LinkedIn

Send 10 connections on LinkedIn a message saying hello. You can either send them a message (here's a sequence we recommend) or for better results send them a voice note using the LinkedIn App. For EVEN BETTER RESULTS why not record a 15-30 second personalised video and send it to your prospect.

DAILY MARKETING CHECKLIST #19:

Email Past Prospective Clients

Email 5 customers/clients who you've spoken to in the past 3-6 months who didn't buy from you and check in to see how they are doing.

DAILY MARKETING CHECKLIST #20:

Follow Up

If you've sent out proposals to clients and they've not got back to you, why not call 3 of those prospective clients and book in a follow up meeting. You can track these interactions using a CRM like Insightly.

DAILY MARKETING CHECKLIST #21:

Tweet Tweet!

Prepare 4-7 tweets that you can schedule using Loomly or Buffer for the week ahead.

DAILY MARKETING CHECKLIST #22:

Instagram Carousel Post

Drop an Instagram Carousel post...don't just upload one image though. Instagram allows you to upload up to ten images/ videos in a single post. Suzy @ Bringmeyoga does an amazing job of this.

DAILY MARKETING CHECKLIST #23:

Facebook Group/Page Invitations

Invite 10 people into your Facebook Group and/or to like your Facebook Page.

DAILY MARKETING CHECKLIST #24:

Post on LinkedIn

Drop a post on LinkedIn, make sure you include a photo and then tag 10-20 people in the post who you would like to reply (make sure they're in your network though). Stuck for content ideas try out Answer the Public.

DAILY MARKETING CHECKLIST #25:

LinkedIn Endorsements

Go and Endorse 5 of your connections on LinkedIn - trust me they'll do the same back.

DAILY MARKETING CHECKLIST #26:

Guest Blog Contribution

Contribute an article to another blog (here's several business blogs you can contribute to: Business Insider, Forbes, Fast Company, Entrepreneur, Inc., Venture Beat, Biz Sugar).

DAILY MARKETING CHECKLIST #27:

Facebook Live Video

Do a Facebook Live into your Facebook Group or Facebook Page - stuck for content ideas then check out Answer the Public.

DAILY MARKETING CHECKLIST #28:

Speak at a Local Networking Group

Reach out to your local networking group and see if they are looking for speakers. Be persistent. Ask a friend to refer you to the group host if needs be.

DAILY MARKETING CHECKLIST #29:

Follow Up with Existing Clients

Put a reminder in ToDoIst to follow up with existing and past clients as well as prospects who've shown an interest. You can create a pipeline of leads in a CRM like Insightly to help you to follow up with prospective clients.

DAILY MARKETING CHECKLIST #30:

IGTV (Instagram TV)

Create an IGTV (InstagramTV) video. These can be much longer than videos in posts.

DAILY MARKETING CHECKLIST #31:

Comment on LinkedIn

Jump into LinkedIn and leave comments against the first 10-20 posts in your feed.

DAILY MARKETING CHECKLIST #32:

Google Analytics

Check Google Analytics on your website to see how your website traffic is performing.

DAILY MARKETING CHECKLIST #33:

FreeIndex Reviews

Another great review tool is FreeIndex, setting up an account is totally free. At the very least it's an extra link back to your website.

DAILY MARKETING CHECKLIST #34:

Local Business Awards

Enter your business into the local business awards if there are any going. If you don't have time to do it, engage with a Local PR Expert who can source local awards and write the pitches for you.

DAILY MARKETING CHECKLIST #35:

Competition on Facebook

Start a competition on your Facebook Page. Encourage people to like, comment and share the post, like your page, submit a gif, or anything to engage them.

DAILY MARKETING CHECKLIST #36:

Free Sh*t Giveaway

Do you have a "free thing" that you can give away to prospective clients? I.e. a book, brochure, flyer, business card, branded pen. If so, then which 5-10 people could you give one to. If not, maybe consider making a free gift for prospects.

DAILY MARKETING CHECKLIST #37:

Email/Message/SMS

Send an email/message/SMS to existing/prospective clients (you may need to be a detective and find out on Facebook...or just start asking people next time you see them).

DAILY MARKETING CHECKLIST #38:

Branded Merchandise

Get a T-Shirt designed with your logo/branding on it. Personally I use Printful - the delivery can be slow but the quality of their garments is excellent.

DAILY MARKETING CHECKLIST #39:

Donate a Prize

Donate a prize in your business' name to a local fundraiser.

DAILY MARKETING CHECKLIST #40:

Facebook Ads

Head on over to Facebook's Business Manager and try a paid ad. You never know it might just work! We've also created an introductory Facebook Ads Course for local businesses.

DAILY MARKETING CHECKLIST #41:

Ask for Referrals

Ask your existing clients for referrals. These tend to be the strongest form of marketing going, with the highest conversion rates. Ensure you incentivise the referral and pay your clients 10-20% commission for each successful client signed.

DAILY MARKETING CHECKLIST #42:

Run an Event

Run an event locally where you can showcase what you do. These can be paid or free. They can be too small audiences of 6-10 people or larger events of 50-100 people who fit your target audience. The event can be a short 90-minute seminar up to a day long event. If you want to learn how to promote a local marketing event for your business then check out this video.

DAILY MARKETING CHECKLIST #43:

Send a Video/Voice Memo on LinkedIn

Don't just send a "normal" message to a prospective client on LinkedIn - why not drop them a Voice Memo using the LinkedIn Mobile App or maybe even create a 15-20 second personalised video for them.

DAILY MARKETING CHECKLIST #44:

Leave a Video Comment on Facebook

If someone is asking for help on social whether it be Facebook, LinkedIn, Twitter or Insta - why not leave them a short video with your answer in the comments rather than just plain text.

DAILY MARKETING CHECKLIST #45:

Create a LinkedIn Poll

Create a Poll on LinkedIn to drive engagement and find out more about your audience.

DAILY MARKETING CHECKLIST #46:

Start a Podcast

Starting a Podcast doesn't have to be hard. Why not download the Anchor.fm App to your mobile phone - it uploads episodes straight up to iTunes, Spotify and a number of well known podcast marketplaces.

DAILY MARKETING CHECKLIST #47:

Promote Another Business Owner

If you can't think of anything to say about your business then promote another fellow business owner on your preferred social media channels.

DAILY MARKETING CHECKLIST #48:

Audible Gift

If someone you know likes audiobooks, why not give them 3 Free Audible Credits. I've actually acquired a client just because I did this once.

DAILY MARKETING CHECKLIST #49:

Send a Gift

Send 3 prospective clients a gift - it could be your book, another author's book, audible credits, or even a link to a video which made you think of them.

DAILY MARKETING CHECKLIST #50:

Professional Headshots

The amount of time I see coaches, consultants and freelancers using selfie-style images on their social media profiles (even LinkedIn), and while I believe in "don't judge a book by it's cover" initial appearances do matter. If you want to be taken seriously do get some headshots taken by a professional photographer, trust be it really makes the difference to your credibility as a serious business owner.

BONUS #2

5 LEVELS OF MARKET SOPHISTICATION

WHEN DO YOUR PROSPECTS BUY FROM YOU?

The principles you are about to learn in this bonus came from the book, "Breakthrough Advertising," written by one of the founding fathers of Direct Response Copywriting, Eugene Schwartz.

If you've not got hold of a copy of Breakthrough Advertising, it is 100% worth it, but it will cost you a few bob.

You can do the "obvious thing" and try to find it on Amazon but it's super expensive. The wise choice would be to go here:

https://breakthroughadvertisingbook.com/

It will cost you $125 (plus $30 shipping to the UK) so about £100.

Expensive for a book but I am happy to provide a personal guarantee that it is one of the best investments you'll ever make in your education around advertising and direct response copywriting. Bar doing Fearless Business, naturally

This one model that I am about to walk you through came

out of that book. I've adapted it slightly, bringing it into the 21st Century (yes, the original book was written by a grey-haired chap in 1967) so it works better for the sorts of clients which we work with including, but not exclusively, coaches, consultants and freelancers

Essentially, this is a very simple model, which explains how to understand and speak to your audience better.

Applying these principles will enable you to avoid all the "buy my sh*t" marketing that seems to be prevalent in the internet marketing age. And don't play stupid, you all know what I'm talking about. You will invariably see it every day on Facebook, Twitter and LinkedIn. You may even be responsible for some of it yourself.

Believe it or not, we've all been there. Even I've been there and done that kind of marketing. It's not pretty, but nowadays people see right through it, but we do NOT want to be that person.

There's a much better way of appealing to our target audiences' wants and desires.

Before I demonstrate the five levels of market sophistication you've got to understand some prerequisites.

THE PREREQUISITES

You've got to know exactly who your target market is, and you've got to understand exactly where it is that they hang out.

What do I mean by that?

Your target market, let's say, for example, is middle-aged men; what sort of things are middle-aged men into?

That will indicate where they might hang out. What I mean by 'where they hang out' in the modern era of internet marketing they WILL BE online somewhere. That's how most marketing works these days. It could be physical, it could be digital, it could be online, it could be he still reads magazines and books, he might listen to audiobooks, or regularly reads the news.

From here you can get more specific. If he's online, what is his preferred platform, is he on Facebook, LinkedIn, the BBC Website etc?

Now we'll dig a third layer deep. If he's on Facebook, which groups is he a member of? What pages does he like? What does he post on his timeline?

You must keep drilling down into exactly who your target market is, where do they hang out, what sort of people and things are they interacting with.

I call these the clues.

These clues help you to understand exactly which level of sophistication your intended audience is at and how to attract them into your ecosystem, so they get curious and want to find out more about your solution.

The other thing is to understand exactly how they FEEL right now.

Your successful middle-aged man who works in the city, who is climbing the career ladder, he's going to be feeling very different to a middle-aged man who is slightly overweight and not fulfilling his career needs.

You've got to understand exactly how he feels to understand where they are in their levels of market sophistication and readiness to buy your product or service.

Market sophistication IS NOT about their level of education, it's about your understanding of their needs; in short empathy.

If you understand how they feel, you're going have a better understanding of their needs, and it's those needs which lead to their collective desire. The collective desire is the transformation of moving from A to B.

In the example I've given, our middle-aged man wants the six-pack back which he had in his twenties.

In one statement you've now identified your target market and what his collective desire is, and from here, you can start to understand how sophisticated a buyer he is and whether he's ready to buy your product specifically.

I'm going to go through each of the 5 Levels of Market Sophistication with a few bullet points, to explain exactly what I mean.

LEVEL 1 – PROBLEM UNAWARE

You now know who your target market is, you know what their collective desire is. However, your target market does not.

They don't know what their problem is, but it's worth remembering there are varying degrees of awareness (or lack of it) at this stage.

They might have no idea about whether they've got a problem, or they might have a slight inkling that they've got a problem, however, whatever's going on is not really on their agenda

When we talk about the problem with them it's not like it's non-existent, it might be there, it's just they're not ready to do anything about it...yet!

The collective desire hinges around the intention to do something about the problem.

If you put your solution, your brand, your product or your price in front of them at this early stage, they're going to be completely blind to it. They have no awareness that they've even got a problem, so they're certainly not looking for a solution.

If you're doing "buy my sh*t" style marketing, and you're getting no responses, it's because you're putting your message in front of an audience who simply doesn't care about your message and are nowhere near ready to buy from you (or anyone) right now.

Right now, they require education to demonstrate to them that they might have a problem.

How do you do that?

You use the art of storytelling. When you're talking about your middle-aged man, you introduce your prospective audience to a story about Fred. Fred is 53, his confidence is at an all-time low, he's two stone overweight and so on.

This engages your audience, especially those who are like Fred.

What's happening is somebody reading that post will be

thinking, "There's a couple of things in there which are kind of like where I'm at. I didn't realise that my weight impacted my confidence."

You're just educating somebody by holding the mirror up and saying, "Hey, we're over here, look, we've got some interesting stuff to say."

Level two is where your audience becomes more problem aware. Moving through the scale of initiative from one to 10, on the acuteness of your prospect's level of awareness around their problem.

LEVEL 2 – PROBLEM AWARE

Now you will have received an acknowledgement of the problem from your audience. They're not blissfully going around burying their head in the sand anymore. There may even be a bit of a desire to think about doing something about the problem.

However, level two audiences feel overwhelmed with whatever the situation is that they're currently in.

Level two audiences don't know where to start in resolving that problem. They're just wandering around feeling a bit down. They don't understand why they feel like this or know what's led to them feeling like this.

They're looking for a bit of positive reassurance and hope the some of that overwhelm can be taken away and affirmed that what they're feeling is perfectly normal.

What is clear is that there is now a positive intention to do something.

The action point at this level is to begin to introduce basic education in the form of attraction advertising.

You can put something more specific in front of them. This is where marketing assets come into their own. Marketing assets in the form of lead magnets to show level two audiences five to ten things that they could start doing to resolve the problem they are now aware that they are experiencing.

Make sure that there's very little friction in delivering the education. These five to ten things that we're showing them must be very simple things that they could do today or tomorrow.

I worked with a personal trainer. Before we started working together, I wanted a simple plan to lose a bit of weight. I'd put on two and a half stone as a keen swimmer and was eating far too much

All I wanted was to rebalance my body and lose a bit of bulk.

The personal trainer offered me a gem of a PDF guide – "10 Ways to Lose Weight". When he gave it to me, he said, "There are ten things in here, which you could do, you don't have to do them all."

I picked out four things:

- Eat the healthiest thing on the menu, I was travelling a lot and going out and having meals with people and eating rubbish. I chose to eat the healthiest thing on the menu from that point forward.
- Ditch the caffeine. I stopped drinking coffee. I've no clue

about the science but it was easy enough to do.

- And the third thing that I chose - reduced sugar intake. I pretty much tried to cut it out entirely.
- Do 20 minutes of extra exercise per session.

And hey-presto, within two months, I'd lost two stone. That built up my trust in my personal trainer. Eventually, I ended up moving through levels three, four and five and becoming his client. The PDF was completely free. As was his consultation. Did I need him further? I'd achieved my goal.

We moved onto some more structured exercises and keeping my body balanced.

His free educational lead magnet gently moved me through the levels of my readiness to buy. Here's where a "low friction" five or ten simple things they could start doing to resolve the problem builds trust and is free.

There's very little resistance. That's what you must create for level two audiences.

Remember they're feeling overwhelmed; you must keep resistance as low as you possibly can.

Now your prospect is starting to move to a place where their desire to change their current circumstances is much more acute. They are in a place where they start to search for solutions.

LEVEL 3 – SOLUTION AWARE

As audiences become more solution aware, they begin to search for specific solutions on Google.

They're starting to educate themselves around what the options are and what products or services might be available to help facilitate change in their current circumstances.

By now they will have narrowed their search down to three or four different businesses, coaches or consultants, and hopefully, you are on the shortlist. You want to proactively be showing a level three audience inside your inner circle.

How you do that is by saying, "Well, hey, look, we've built a community around this subject, why don't you join our Facebook group?" or "Listen, we've got this programme which might help you, but I want to see whether it's a good fit or not. How do you feel about taking the next step?"

Remember low resistance and low friction.

Make it super easy for your intended audience to hop on a call for 15 minutes or answer some simple questions in a messenger chat.

But what are you DEFINITELY NOT going to do?

Please note: this is super, super important.

If your intended audience is at level one, level two or level three you DEFINITELY DO NOT introduce your brand, your product, or your price.

I repeat; up to level three, you DO NOT talk about your brand, your product or your prices. You may SUBTLY introduce it.

On your lead magnet, for example, maybe pop your logo on there, subtle but inoffensive. But let's keep it personal. Put your headshot and a bit of personal bio about yourself. But do not sell your products or mention price.

If you push level four marketing on anyone from level one to three, you are being exactly that; far too pushy.

Buy my sh*t marketing and giving them too much too soon will scare your prospect off and they'll run for the hills.

LEVEL 4 – BRAND AWARE

Now you've got your target market inside your inner circle. They're in your Facebook group or connected with them on LinkedIn. Maybe they've come along to an event which you've hosted. You may have even had the pleasure of sitting a consultation with them.

Level four audiences have nearly everything they need to make a buying decision.

It is worth remembering that moving your intended audience through levels one, two and three can take weeks, months or even years.

This is where the biggest mistake happens in modern marketing. People are too keen to take people's money and so rush the marketing and sales processes.

It's not until level four that they're going to be thinking about whether working with you is a good fit. They're still deciding whether they prefer you over your competition.

I repeat; even at level four if you're too pushy, and your competition isn't, it's likely that you might turn your prospect off and they'll go to your competition.

The nuances of marketing and sales processes are incredibly subtle. So subtle in fact that most people overlook it because they're too focussed on taking people's money.

When YOU need the sale it's no longer about working within your prospect's best interests. When YOU NEED the sale, it's about you. And if your sales process is all about you, then you're always going to lose the sale. It's always going to be a disappointment for both you and your prospect.

It's a lose-lose situation.

If it's all about you then the one thing which they lack is the confidence in your ability to deliver what you say you're going to deliver.

At this stage in the customer's journey results, social proof, case studies, testimonials and client success stories are vital.

If you're not getting Google reviews, if you're not getting video testimonials, if you're not taking snapshots of client wins, and putting them somewhere on your website and shouting about them or making it easy for your audience to see them you are losing the battle.

Load all your testimonials onto a client success page on your website and send your prospective client a link with all the social proof on it.

Even then, there's a potential that you're not going to build up the confidence in your prospect to enable them to take that next step with you and buy your product.

The key to winning this battle is in having a thorough and whole process and to assume a position of leadership throughout the sequence of the five levels.

If you lose leadership at any point you will lose the sale.

Level four audiences are primed to receiving an offer from you. You must put a compelling offer in front of them. Don't assume at any stage, they're just going to turn around and say, "Here's my money, I'm in."

Sometimes it happens. But 95% of the time it doesn't.

Your audience needs to be led throughout the entire process, including when they're about to make that buying decision. If they're not asking the right questions, you have got to lead them into asking the right questions.

If they're missing a key piece of information, you've got to lead them and give them that piece of information.

If the decision is that they need to go to your competition instead of you, if you can't deliver what you say you can do, then you have to give them what they need.

Assume that position of leadership, take the moral high ground and give them the contact details of your competition. I cannot stress how important this is.

I will say it again; you have to be the one assuming that position of leadership and put the right offer in front of them, even if that offer is NOT you.

Only then can you move up to the final level of initiative.

LEVEL 5 – PRODUCT AND PRICE AWARE

Your target market has already made her final buying decision.

At this point, what they're most interested to know about are the features of your product, how it's delivered, and how much it's going to cost.

Don't assume they automatically know what the next steps in your process are.

She might know what your product is, what result it produces and how much it costs. But don't assume she will automatically be going to take those next steps and sign up.

You must lead take her by the hand and take her through your process.

What this sounds like is, "Awesome, this is going to be great for you. So, here is what's going to happen next, I'm going to send over the agreement which you need to sign within the next couple of days."

If she needs to think about it. "Great, I would do the same, it's a big decision. How about we book in a follow-up call in two days where we can discuss that and you can tell me whether it's a yes or no?"

Ask her what she needs to see from you to help make her final decision.

I see far too many coaches, consultants and freelancers hiding behind proposals.

When a prospective client says, "Can you send me some more information?" at the end of a sales call my standard reply is,

"What do you need to know from me to make the decision now?" or "Ask me the questions now, and let's skip the proposal because I don't want to write it and I doubt you'll want to read it!"

Often, prospects they don't know what questions they've got to ask. They need a prompt; some coaching through the final part of the decision-making process.

Don't talk too much. Interject 8-10 second periods of silence into the sales conversation to give your prospect time to process the information you've given them.

If you're moving through the five levels via messenger, or even on a call, leave moments of reflection. It may feel awkward, but rather than bombarding them with words or messages or proposals and then following up aggressively, people need time and space to make their buying decisions.

Interject with moments of silence on purpose using that position of leadership that you've assumed at strategic points in the process.

You've got to be patient, listen to their concerns your prospect raises and address them. Don't feel you've got to justify your position using features of your products or services. Keep your prospect focussed on outcomes and results.

Only when you've gone through all five levels of initiative, can you close the deal. Closing the deal sounds like, "Great. So, here are the next steps. You will need to sign the agreement which I will send over after the call. Can I take your credit card details to process the deposit? Can we book in your first coaching session?" Or whatever it might be. Close the deal.

A few things to note (and this is just a little bit of a recap).

At no point in the examples of the five levels I've given you will you have seen any kind of "buy my sh*t" type marketing.

These five levels are the five fundamental steps of advertising and marketing. If you understand these five steps, you will understand your audience better, and you will know how to talk to them without doing any kind of "buy my sh*t" marketing at them.

At all stages your content has to be about your prospect, educating your prospect and delivering value to your prospect. As Gary Vaynerchuck puts it, "Jab, Jab, Jab, Right Hook".

Lead them and pull them through your process. This is not about you. This is all about your prospect.

You've got to ensure that the customer journey is seamless, no matter what stage of the buying journey your prospect is at. What I mean by this is you can't just skip stages. Regardless of whether they come in a stage one or two, or stages three or four or five. If they enter your customer journey at stage two, you have to build them up through stages two, three, four and five before you try and close them.

If they come in at stage five, great, it's no build-up, you've just got to close your prospect. But you can't then jump back and do more of the early education either.

If you think they're a stage five buyer and they require extra education then they're either confused or whatever you give them next will confuse them.

You simply can't skip stages; you've got to move your audience through each of those levels of initiative to help them make an educated decision

Secondly, don't assume anything. You cannot assume that your prospects know anything about you or understand your processes. They don't understand what result they're going to get through working with you. They don't know what the next steps are going to be when they say, "Yes!". You've got to assume they know absolutely nothing about you, your business, your solution and your entire process.

However, there is one thing you can assume. And that is a position of leadership throughout.

Remember what I wrote previously about there being a sequence to a customer journey.

It's a linear sequence of steps which you take every prospect through. From the first point of them finding out about you right the way through to the sale, delivery and beyond. It's linear. Consider it to be like a timeline. You can't allow the client to jump backwards and forwards along that line.

Some of you may believe in time travel, but I certainly don't believe in time travel, you can't jump about in time. You must see the customer journey as that sequence of events over time. If somebody asks for a price (remember, level five), and they are only at level one or level two or level three then don't tell them the price. Your prospect must be at level five before you give them the price.

You must lead your prospect, "Okay, well before I give you the price there are a few things which I need to know about you; we've got to see whether it's a good fit."

Assume that position of leadership.

Don't be led by the client.

I haven't mastered marketing by any stretch, but understanding these five levels of market sophistication is one of the reasons why people see my advertising and marketing as successful.

All of my content is about adding value, tapping into people's problems, offering up a solution whether it's mine or somebody else's and taking them through every stage in the process. I'm incredibly patient. I have prospects where it's taken two or even three years before they've signed up and become clients.

This is a long game for me and marketing should be a long game for you too.

If you implement the five levels of market sophistication it should take a long time to convert prospects onto consultations.

It should take a long time to get clients booked on from that very first interaction which you have with them.

It is not a quick process.

It is an effective process though and you must start enjoying the process because it will create consistent results and better clients for your business.

BONUS #3
DO THIS LITTLE EXERCISE

I got one final activity which I wanted to share with you.

I did this while I was out in Cyprus mastermind about three weeks ago. I was on the mastermind with ten butch blokes, like all fitness professionals with massive arms and then little ol' me.

This activity made all of us cry and turn into gibbering blubbery messes, so I'm just giving you a bit of a heads up in advance. If you don't want to partake that's fine.

From a marketing perspective, it will get you to rethink the content you're putting out – from a personal development perspective this will be huge for you.

Whoever wants to play the game, get stuck in.

Think of a person who you love, the first person that comes to mind, and write them a letter. I want you to spend five minutes writing that letter.

I'm about to demonstrate the power of words.

Somebody you love, write them a letter, the first thing that comes to your mind, don't even think about it. Just write it down on a bit of paper. Just scribble, start writing some sentences down. The person could be your partner, mother, brother, sister, aunt, uncle, dead relative, whatever it doesn't matter, write the letter.

What I'd also encourage you to do once you've finished your letter is to get a beautiful piece of paper at some point, write it down neatly and give it to the person to whom you wrote it.

Here's my letter. I wasn't going to share it to you, but I thought you'd struggle to see my point without it. So, here it is:

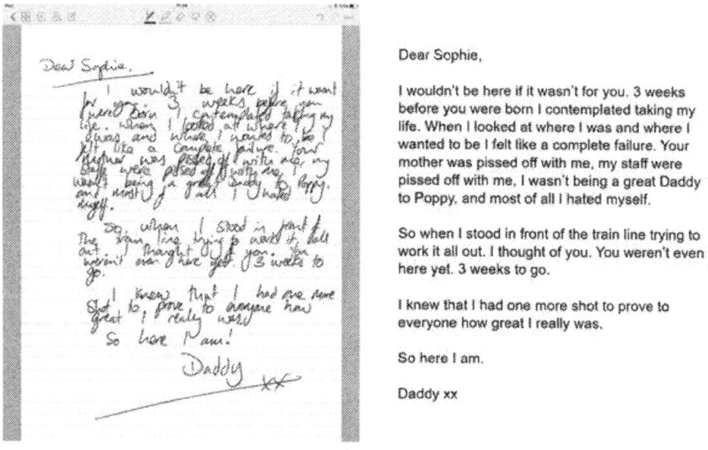

Dear Sophie,

I wouldn't be here if it wasn't for you. 3 weeks before you were born I contemplated taking my life. When I looked at where I was and where I wanted to be I felt like a complete failure. Your mother was pissed off with me, my staff were pissed off with me, I wasn't being a great Daddy to Poppy, and most of all I hated myself.

So when I stood in front of the train line trying to work it all out. I thought of you. You weren't even here yet. 3 weeks to go.

I knew that I had one more shot to prove to everyone how great I really was.

So here I am.

Daddy xx

My letter to my youngest daughter, Sophie

Please, I beg of you, think about the content you're writing. No more of this bland, vanilla bullshit, boring content. Let's entertain some people, write some great, entertaining and engaging content.

"Your business is great, so shout about it, please!"

NEXT STEPS

If you want a FREE 30-Minute Diagnostic Call, then please follow the link below and complete my short application form:

https://fearless.biz/app

And if you've got a copy of *Marketing Machine* and not yet left a review, please put your hand up.

Oh! That hurts!!

Please don't forget to LEAVE A REVIEW on Amazon. It helps enourmously with sales.

Email me, robin@robinwaite.com if you'd like to know more about what we get up to in my Fearless Business Accelerator as well.

ABOUT THE AUTHOR

The first job I took was a paper round, the longest one in the village I lived in, and it paid the most amount of money. The tips I collected every Christmas for four years were bigger than any of the other delivery boys and girls. It meant I could afford to buy two or three CDs a week whereas most of my peers struggled to afford one or two per month.

Soon I was investing my paper-round money in second-hand CDs and selling them at my school to my peers so that I could afford the latest albums and the best Sony hi-fi I could afford.

Not knowing what business I wanted to start; at 18 I worked as a systems analyst, which gave me an enormous insight into systems and processes but my methods resulted in staff in the company I worked at being made redundant. The money wasn't great, so by 22, I'd started a great sideline selling grade-B laptops. I made enough money to quit my job and, in one summer, made over £40,000. Mostly cash (declared, I might add) but that money was sat on the end of my bed. I did what any savvy 22-year-old would have done and bought a car, and booked a holiday with my girlfriend to Florida to see her brother.

While out in Florida I got a call from an old colleague to start up a creative agency.

My design agency wasn't like any other; ordinarily, a new client would submit a request-for-quote, which would trigger this game of "design agency ping-pong." This involved months of back and forth between the agency and customer. I knew there had to be a better way than doing everything remotely; so I created a series of intensive 1-to-1 workshops.

The workshops involved the client working directly with a strategy expert and either a developer or designer – depending on whether it was a website or branding workshop. Typically, this would take 1-2 days.

Logo design, for example; is a process which can take up to eight weeks to create a professional logo. This lengthy process is down to poor communication or lack of time. We charged £60 per hour, and a logo might generate 8-10 hours of chargeable work during that eight-week game of design agency ping-pong.

I invited the client in for a one-to-one, 1-day branding workshop. The process had seven steps with clearly defined outcomes. We charged a fixed price which was £1,495, nearly three times the hourly rate previously charged. I offered a 100% money back guarantee. I did the same with websites and created a 2-day prototyping workshop. It started to slot into place.

Four years later.

After speeding down Frocester Hill at 50+ mph, I split off from my cycling club buddies and found myself stood next to a railway line. All I could think was, "I want more, I want to go faster!" A train whooshed past. My thoughts turned to, "What if I had stood in front of that train?" quickly countered by, "Well, I wasn't! So, something had to change." – I realised that something was missing in my life and I had to act.

After talking things through with my life coach, Michael Serwa, we realised that I wasn't passionate about building websites or designing logos, I had created a "job" for myself. However, I loved working with people, teaching them, creating products for them, building assets, and creating systems so they could charge more.

Michael said to me during one session, "Robin, it sounds to me like you're coaching!"

I spent three months rebranding and relaunched myself as a business coach. I had set a goal. I wanted to get ten clients within my first year. I created 14 clients in 6 weeks. At the age of 35 I am now running a 6-figure coaching business with great clients, and it is thanks to Michael, my coach, for kicking me into action and giving me the belief that I could do it.

Now, I coach other businesses owners and managers to do what I did. My niche is professional service businesses. From creative agencies turning over £20k+ per year to large accountancy firms turning over £2m+. I have created a number of my coaching tools to facilitate my fortnightly or monthly meetings with my clients.

I get a tremendous sense of achievement when I see my clients' businesses prosper and I have a goal to help 10,000 business owners in the next five years to double their turnover within six months using my tools. I can't do this all on a one-to-one basis, so I have created a number of coaching tools and programmes, and deliver regular talks and workshops to enable me to achieve my goal.

https://fearless.biz/

FEARLESS BUSINESS

The 12-Week Fearless Business Accelerator is for anyone who is serious about growing their business, and potentially doubling your turnover and profit.

You will become part of a family where I am the mother hen - I am incredibly proud of my brood whenever they have amazing wins, and lightbulb moments!!!

There are a number of things you will get access to:

- The 12-Week Fearless Business Accelerator
- Online Portal & Workbook
- Weekly Call - Q&A
- Accountability in the Fearless Business Facebook Group
- Message me anytime you like (don't take the p*ss) with you challenges and I'll jump on it ASAP.
- Turbo Calls for extra Momentum
- Pre-release copies of future books, before anyone else.
- Access to my little black book of contacts

You can apply to join at any time, it all starts with a **FREE 30-Minute Diagnostic Call:**

https://fearless.biz/app

Book your call now! What are you waiting for?

READING LIST

Title	What It'sAbout
Think and Grow Rich Napoleon Hill	We can learn to think like the rich we can discover wealth and success.
Built to Sell John Warrilow	Creating a Business That Can Thrive Without You
Go For No Richard Fenton and Andrea Waltz	Yes is the Destination, No is How You Get There
The Startup Coach Carl Reader	Other books help you talk the talk; the Teach Yourself Coach books will help you walk the walk.
The Lean Startup Eric Reis	How Today's Entrepreneurs Use Continuous Innovation to Create Radically Successful Businesses
The Prosperous Coach Steve Chandler and Rich Litvin	Increase Income and Impact for You and Your Clients
How to Be F*cking Awesome Dan Meredith	A kick up the backside to finally launch that business, start a new project you've been putting off or just become all round awesome.
24 Assets Daniel Priestley	Create a digital, scalable, valuable and fun business that will thrive in a fast changing world
The Phoenix Project Gene Kim and Kevin Behr	A Novel About IT, DevOps, and Helping Your Business Win
Principled Selling David Tovey	How to Win More Business Without Selling Your Soul
Elon Musk Ashlee Vance	How the Billionaire CEO of SpaceX and Tesla is Shaping our Future
From Good to Amazing Michael Serwa	No Bullshit Tips for The Life You Always Wanted

Title	What It'sAbout
The Goal Jeff Cox, Eliyahu Goldratt	A Process of Ongoing Improvement
The Big Leap Gay Hedricks	Conquer Your Hidden Fear and Take Life to the Next Level
Sell or Be Sold Grant Cardone	How to Get Your Way in Business and Life
Flash Boys Michael Lewis	If you thought Wall Street was about alpha males standing in trading pits hollering at each other, think again
Life Leverage Rob Moore	How to Get More Done in Less Time, Outsource Everything & Create Your Ideal Mobile Lifestyle
Online Business Startup Robin Waite	The entrepreneur's guide to launching a fast, lean and profitable online venture
Outliers Malcolm Gladwell	The Story of Success

Printed in Poland
by Amazon Fulfillment
Poland Sp. z o.o., Wrocław

22665530R00060